SWU-GEN-003

UNIFORMS OF FRENCH ARMIES 1750-1870 VOL. 2

IN THE ART OF JOB

SOLDIERSHOP PUBLISHING

AUTHOR

Jacques Marie Gaston Onfroy de Bréville, known by the pen name **Job** after his initials (25 November 1858, Bar-le-Duc – 15 September 1931, Neuilly-sur-Seine) was a famous French artist and illustrator that maintained a keen taste for military, patriotic and nationalistic subjects.

PUBLISHING'S NOTE

None of **unpublished** images or text of our book may be reproduced in any format without the expressed written permission of Soldiershop.com when not indicate as marked with license creative commons 3.0 or 4.0. The publisher remains to disposition of the possible having right for all the doubtful sources images or not identifies. Our trademark: Soldiershop Publishing ©, The names of our series: Soldiers&Weapons, Battlefield, War in colour, PaperSoldiers, Soldiershop e-book etc. are herein © by Soldiershop.com.

NOTE ABOUT BOOK PRINTING BEFORE 1925

This book may contain text or images coming from a reproduction of a book published before 1925 (over seventy years ago). No effort has been made to modernize or standardize the spelling used in the original text, so this book may have occasional imperfections such as missing or blurred pages, poor pictures, errant marks, etc. that were either part of the original artifact, or were introduced by the scanning process. We believe this work is culturally important, and despite the imperfections, have elected to bring it back into print (digital and/or paper) as part of our continuing commitment to the preservation of printed works worldwide. We appreciate your understanding of the imperfections in the preservation process, and hope you enjoy this valuable book. Now this book is purpose re-built and is proof-read and re-type set from the original to provide an outstanding experience of reflowing text, also for an ebook reader. However Soldiershop publishing added, enriched, revised and overhauled the text, images, etc. of the cover and the book. Therefore, the job is now to all intents and purposes a derivative work, and the added, new and original parts of the book are the copyright of Soldiershop. On this second unpublished part of the book none of images or text may be reproduced in any format without the expressed written permission of Soldiershop. Almost many of the images of our books and prints are taken from original first edition prints or books that are no longer in copyright and are therefore public domain. We have been a specialized bookstore for a long time so we (and several friends antiquarian booksellers) have readily available a lot of ancient, historical and illustrated books not in copyright. Each of our prints, art designs or illustrations is either our own creation, or a fully digitally restoration by our computer artists, or non copyrighted images. All of our prints are "tagged" with a registered digital copyright. Soldiershop remains to disposition of the possible having right for all the doubtful sources images or not identifies.

LICENSES COMMONS

Much of the text in this book are from the *"Memoirs of the Empress Catherine II., by Catherine II, Empress of Russia"* This book is for the use of anyone anywhere at no cost and with almost no restrictions whatsoever. You may copy it, give it away or re-use it under the terms of the similar creative commons License. This book may utilize material marked with license creative commons 3.0 or 4.0 (CC BY 4.0), (CC BY-ND 4.0), (CC BY-SA 4.0) or (CC0 1.0). We give appropriate attribution credit and indicate if change were made below in the acknowledgements field.

ACKNOWLEDGEMENTS

A Special Thanks to NYPL and other institutions for their kindly permission to use some images of his archives, collections or books used in our book.

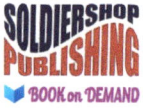

Title: **UNIFORMS OF FRENCH ARMIES 1750-1870 VOL. 2** - The Napoleonic army In the art of Job
By Luca Stefano Cristini, color plates by Job. Serie edit by Luca S. Cristini. First edition by Soldiershop. July 2019
Cover & Art Design: Luca S. Cristini. ISBN code: 978-88-93274357
Published by Luca Cristini Editore, via Orio 35/4- 24050 Zanica (BG) ITALY. www.soldiershop.com

UNIFORMS OF FRENCH ARMIES 1750-1870 Vol. 2

THE NAPOLEONIC ARMY IN THE ART OF JOB

Luca Stefano Cristini

THE WONDERFUL WORLD OF THE JOB'S SOLDIERS

In this book are present the development and complexity of France's uniforms, from the Louis XV era just to Second Empire of Napoleon III. All the subjects are seen through the eyes of a great French artist. Jacques Marie Gaston Onfroy de Bréville, well known by the pen name Job after his initials (1858-1931).
The serie is published on 3 volume that includes about 200 and more wonderful original illustrations of uniforms from the 18th century to Napoleonic era and just to 1870 about.
This book presents pictorial documentation of the appearance of French soldiers throughout the period with the support of short essays on France's military history. The particularly well-executed original Job's illustrations, slightly restored by our graphic artist are presented to the general public here for the first time. Job's plates shows how the Royal and (after) Imperial French Army, time and again, was a decisive factor in the story of Europe.

In the second volume of the serie we present the French soldiers during the glorious years of Napoleonic era.

IL MERAVIGLIOSO MONDO DEI SOLDATI DI JOB

In questo libro presentiamo il fascino e la storia delle uniformi francesi, dalle armate di Luigi XV a Napoleone III e il Secondo Impero. Tutti soggetti sono opera di un solo grande artista: Jacques Marie Gaston Onfroy de Bréville (1858-1931), meglio noto con lo pseudonimo di Job, dalle iniziali del suo nome. Tutte le tavole fanno parte di una collezione di oltre duecento disegni a colori, e sono presentati su tre volumi. Si tratta come è noto del periodo più glorioso della storia di Francia, e la maestria di Job , fervente patriota oltre che grande artista, rende particolare merito a queste tavole capolavoro. Questo lavoro è anche il primo mai edito in Italia.
In questo secondo volume sono trattate le uniformi indossate durante i circa 15 anni dell'era napoleonica. Buona lettura e soprattutto buona visione

Portrait of Napoleon I at Wagram (1809) paint by Horace Vernet

SHORT HISTORY OF THE FRENCH ARMY

THE FRENCH SOLDIER OF FIRST EMPIRE

The Napoleonic Era saw French power and influence reach immense heights, even though the period of domination was relatively brief. In the century and a half preceding the Revolutionary Era, France had transformed demographic leverage to military and political weight; the French population was 19 million in 1700, but this had grown to over 29 million in 1800, much higher than that of most other European powers. These interesting numbers permitted France to raise armies at a rapid pace should the need arise. Furthermore, military innovations carried out during the Revolution and the Consulate, evidenced by improvements in artillery and cavalry capabilities on top of better army and staff organization, gave the French army a decisive advantage in the initial stages of the Napoleonic Wars. Another ingredient of success was Napoleon Bonaparte himself—intelligent, charismatic, and a military genius, Napoleon absorbed the latest military theories of the day and applied them in the battlefield with deadly effect.

Napoleon inherited an army that was based on conscription and used huge masses of poorly trained troops, which could usually be readily replaced. By 1805 the French Army was a truly lethal force, with many in its ranks veterans of the French Revolutionary Wars. Two years of constant drilling for an invasion of England helped to build a well-trained, well-led army. The Imperial Guard served as an example for the rest of the army and consisted of Napoleon's best handpicked soldiers. Napoleon's huge losses suffered during the disastrous Russian campaign would have destroyed any professional commander of the day, but those losses were quickly replaced with new draftees. After Napoleon, nations planned for huge armies with professional leadership and a constant supply of new soldiers, which had huge human costs when improved weapons like the rifled musket replaced the inaccurate muskets of Napoleon's day during the American Civil War.

This large size came at a cost, as the logistics of feeding a huge army made them especially dependent on supplies. Most armies of the day relied on the supply-convoy system established during the Thirty Years' War by Gustavus Adolphus. This limited mobility, since the soldiers had to wait for the convoys, but it did keep possibly mutinous troops from deserting, and thus helped preserve an army's composure. However, Napoleon's armies were so large that feeding them using the old method proved ineffective, and consequently, French troops were allowed to live off the land. Infused with new concepts of nation and service. Napoleon often attempted to wage decisive, quick campaigns so that he could allow his men to live off the land. The French army did use a convoy system, but it was stocked with very few days worth of food; Napoleon's troops were expected to march quickly, effect a decision on the battlefield, then disperse to feed. For the Russian campaign, the French did store 24 days' worth of food before beginning active operations, but this campaign was the exception, not the rule.

Napoleon's biggest influence in the military sphere was in the conduct of warfare. Weapons and technology remained largely static through the Revolutionary and Napoleonic eras, but 18th-century operational strategy underwent massive restructuring. Sieges became infrequent to the point of near-irrelevance, a new emphasis arose towards the destruction of enemy armies as well as their outmaneuvering, and invasions of enemy territory occurred over broader fronts, thus introducing a plethora of strategic opportunities that made wars costlier and, just as importantly, more decisive. Defeat for a European power now meant much more than losing isolated enclaves. Near-Carthaginian treaties intertwined whole national efforts—social, political, economic, and militaristic—into gargantuan collisions that severely upset international conventions as understood at the time. Napoleon's initial success sowed the seeds for his downfall. Not used to such catastrophic defeats in the rigid power system of 18th-century Europe, many nations found existence under the French yoke difficult, sparking revolts, wars, and general instability that plagued the continent until 1815, when the forces of reaction finally triumphed at the Battle of Waterloo.

Until the time of Napoleon, European states employed relatively small armies, made up of both national soldiers and mercenaries. These regulars were highly drilled professional soldiers. Ancien Régime armies could only deploy small field armies due to rudimentary staffs and comprehensive yet cumbersome logistics. Both issues combined to limit field forces to approximately 30,000 men under a single commander.

Military innovators in the mid-18th century began to recognise the potential of an entire nation at war: a "nation in arms".[126]

The scale of warfare dramatically enlarged during the Revolutionary and subsequent Napoleonic Wars. During Europe's major pre-revolutionary war, the Seven Years' War of 1756–1763, few armies ever numbered more than 200,000 with field forces often numbering less than 30,000. The French innovations of separate corps (allowing a single commander to efficiently command more than the traditional command span of 30,000 men) and living off the land (which allowed field armies to deploy more men without requiring an equal increase in supply arrangements such as depots and supply trains) allowed the French republic to field much larger armies than their opponents. Napoleon ensured during the time of the French republic that separate French field armies operated as a single army under his control, often allowing him to substantially outnumber his opponents. This forced his continental opponents to increase the size of their armies as well, moving away from the traditional small, well drilled Ancien Régime armies of the 18th century to mass conscript armies.

The Battle of Marengo, which largely ended the War of the Second Coalition, was fought with fewer than 60,000 men on both sides. The Battle of Austerlitz which ended the War of the Third Coalition involved fewer than 160,000 men. The Battle of Friedland which led to peace with Russia in 1807 involved about 150,000 men.

After these defeats, the continental powers developed various forms of mass conscription to allow them to face France on even terms, and the size of field armies increased rapidly. The battle of Wagram of 1809 involved 300,000 men, and 500,000 fought at Leipzig in 1813, of whom 150,000 were killed or wounded.

About a million French soldiers became casualties (wounded, invalided or killed), a higher proportion than in the First World War. The European total may have reached 5,000,000 military deaths, including disease.[127][128]

France had the second-largest population in Europe by the end of the 18th century (27 million, as compared to Britain's 12 million and Russia's 35 to 40 million).[129] It was well poised to take advantage of the *levée en masse*. Before Napoleon's efforts, Lazare Carnot played a large part in the reorganisation of the French army from 1793 to 1794—a time which saw previous French misfortunes reversed, with Republican armies advancing on all fronts. The French army peaked in size in the 1790s with 1.5 million Frenchmen enlisted although battlefield strength was much less. Haphazard bookkeeping, rudimentary medical support and lax recruitment standards ensured that many soldiers either never existed, fell ill or were unable to withstand the physical demands of soldiering. About 2.8 million Frenchmen fought on land and about 150,000 at sea, bringing the total for France to almost 3 million combatants during almost 25 years of warfare.[23]

Britain had 750,000 men under arms between 1792 and 1815 as its army expanded from 40,000 men in 1793[130] to a peak of 250,000 men in 1813.[21] Over 250,000 sailors served in the Royal Navy. In September 1812, Russia had 900,000 enlisted men in its land forces, and between 1799 and 1815 2.1 million men served in its army. Another 200,000 served in the Russian Navy. Out of the 900,000 men, the field armies deployed against France numbered less than 250,000.

There are no consistent statistics for other major combatants. Austria's forces peaked at about 576,000 (during the War of the Sixth Coalition) and had little or no naval component yet never fielded more than 250,000 men in field armies. After Britain, Austria proved the most persistent enemy of France; more than a million Austrians served during the long wars. Its large army was overall quite homogeneous and solid and in 1813 operated in Germany (140,000 men), Italy and the Balkans (90,000 men at its peak, about 50,000 men during most of the campaigning on these fronts). Austria's manpower was becoming quite limited towards the end of the wars, leading its generals to favour cautious and conservative strategies, to limit their losses.

Prussia never had more than 320,000 men under arms at any time. In 1813–1815, the core of its army (about 100,000 men) was characterised by competence and determination, but the bulk of its forces consisted of second- and third-line troops, as well as militiamen of variable strength. Many of these troops performed reasonably well and often displayed considerable bravery but lacked the professionalism of their regular counterparts and were not as well equipped. Others were largely unfit for operations, except sieges. During the 1813 campaign, 130,000 men were used in the military operations, with 100,000 effectively participating in the main German campaign, and about 30,000 being used to besiege isolated French garrisons.[22]

Spain's armies also peaked at around 200,000 men, not including more than 50,000 guerrillas scattered over Spain. In addition the Maratha Confederation, the Ottoman Empire, Italy, Naples and the Duchy of Warsaw each had more than 100,000 men under arms. Even small nations now had armies rivalling the size of the Great Powers' forces of past wars but most of these were poor quality forces only suitable for garrison duties. The size of their combat forces remained modest yet they could still provide a welcome addition to the major powers. The percentage of French troops in the Grande Armee which Napoleon led into Russia was about 50% while the French allies also provided a significant contribution to the French forces in Spain. As these small nations joined the coalition forces in 1813–1814, they provided a useful addition to the coalition while depriving Napoleon of much needed manpower.

THE ARTIS JOB

Job pencil self portrait

Jacques Marie Gaston Onfroy de Bréville, known by the pen name **Job** after his initials (25 November 1858, Bar-le-Duc – 15 September 1931, Neuilly-sur-Seine) was a French artist and illustrator. His father opposed his entry to thé École des beaux-arts after graduating from the Collège Stanislas. He therefore joined the French army, but returned to Paris in 1882. In the intervening period, he maintained a keen taste for military, patriotic and nationalistic subjects. He finally joined the École des beaux-arts and exhibited at the 1886 'Salon des artistes français', receiving a mixed reception. He therefore began a career as an illustrator, contributing caricatures to *La Caricature* and to *La Lune*. However, he is best known for his illustrations for children's books, most frequently for texts by Georges Montorgueil. His major colour compositions contributed to the cult of 'heroes of the nation' such as Napoleon I and Joachim Murat. Several of his illustrations appear in *La Vieille Garde impériale* (*The Old Imperial Guard*), published in 1932 by Alfred Mame and fils de Tours. His eye for detail can be seen in *L'Épopée du costume militaire français* - even in works intended for children, he tried to reproduce uniforms with extreme precision.

His best known works are *Murat, Le Grand Napoléon des petits enfants, Jouons à l'histoire, Louis XI, Napoléon, Bonaparte* and *Les Gourmandises de Charlotte*. He also illustrated the life of George Washington and was well known in the USA. He was a Sociétaire of the 'humoristes' and exhibited with the Incoherents. His studio has been reconstructed at the musée de Metz

French Imperial guard in campaign, by Job.

THE PLATES
Vol. 3

TROMPETTE DU 21ᵉ DRAGONS (COMPAGNIE D'ÉLITE) (1802-1812).

1802-1812 Trumpet of the 21ˢᵗ elite dragoon Regt. company

1803 1st Remoise guard of honour

Garde d'honneur de Lyon. — Giberne de cavalier.

Garde d'honneur de Lyon. — Sabre de cavalier.

Cuirasse du colonel Lataye, commandant le 10ᵉ Régiment de Cuirassiers (1803-1806).
(Musée de Bar-le-Duc).

1804-1814 Honor guard of Lyon cavalry gibern and sword, 1803-1806 Cuirasse of Colonel Lataye, commander of the 10th Regt. of cuirassiers

POMPIER DE PARIS

(Premier Empire)

1803 Paris fireman

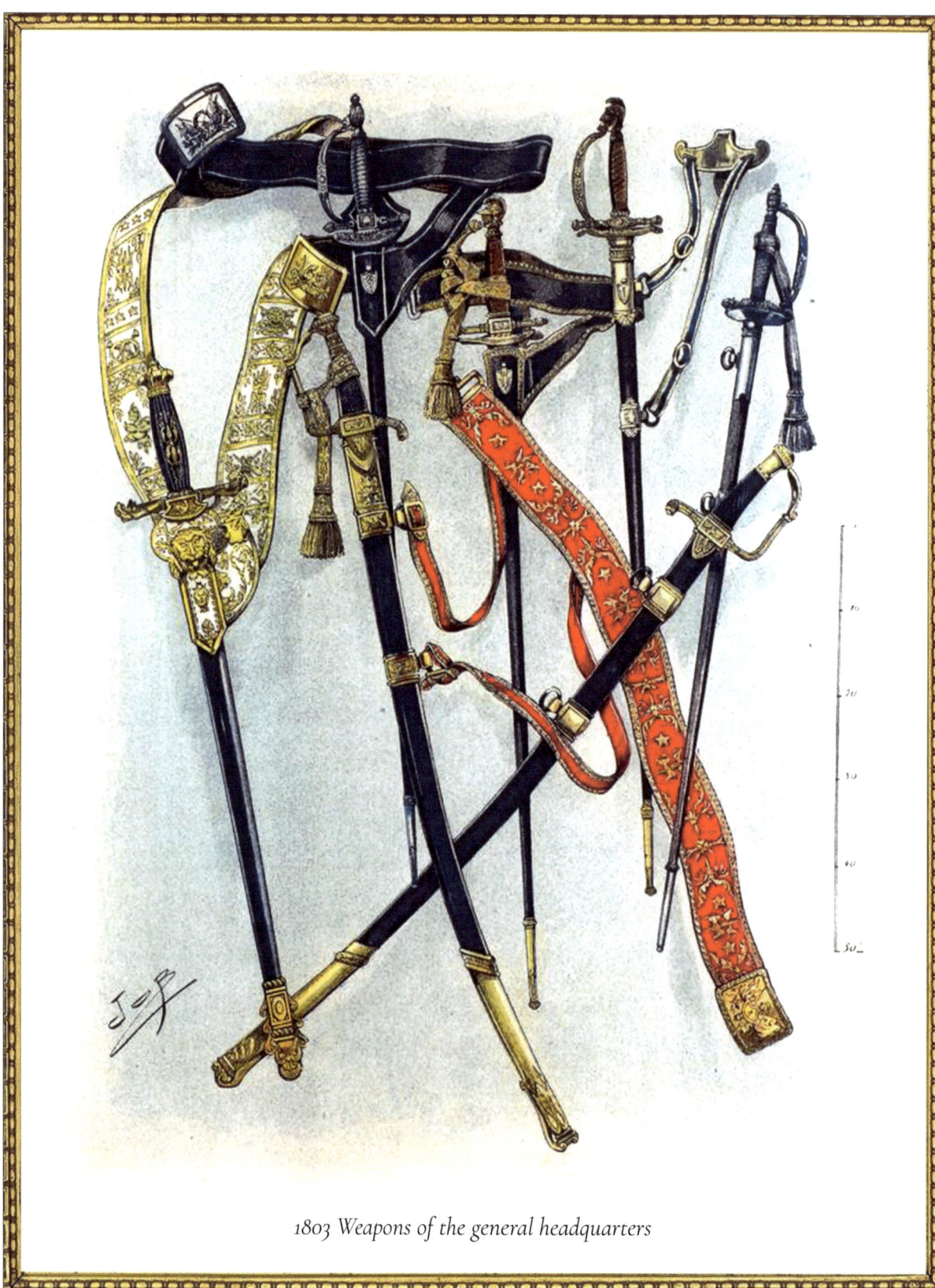

1803 Weapons of the general headquarters

1803-1812 Line infantry and infantry grenadier

GÉNÉRAL RETRAITÉ, COMMISSAIRE DES GUERRES ET OFFICIER DE HUSSARDS RÉFORMÉS. An XII.

1804 General and veterans from An XII

ÉLÈVES DE L'ÉCOLE DES TROMPETTES DE SAINT-GERMAIN
(PREMIER EMPIRE)

1804 Students of the trumpet school of Saint-Germain

1804-1814 Honor guard of Lyon: cavalry trumpet

1804-1814 Honor guard of Lyon: drummer and sapper

1804-1814 Honor guard of Lyon: cavalry

1804-1814 Honor guard of Lyon: general

ASPIRANT DE 1ʳᵉ CLASSE   ÉQUIPAGE DE HAUT-BORD   (COMPAGNIE D'ABORDAGE)
(1804-1814)

1804-1814 Navy crew

1804-1815 Courier from Neuchatel

1804-1815 Light infantry musicians

CUIRASSIER EN VOYAGE. — 5me RÉGIMENT
(PREMIER EMPIRE)

1805 Cuirassier of 5th Regt. in campaign dress

GARDE DÉPARTEMENTALE DE PARIS
CAPORAL PORTE-GUIDON
(an XIII)

1805 Departament guard of Paris

SOLDAT DU TRAIN DES ÉQUIPAGES

Deuxième Bataillon

(Premier Empire)

1805 Driver of equipment train

ÉLÈVE DE L'ÉCOLE PRÉPARATOIRE DE LA FLÈCHE

(Premier Empire)

1805 Young soldat in the prepatory school of La Fleche

SAPEUR DU 1ᵉʳ REGIMENT DE DRAGONS (1806-1811)

1805-1811 Sapper of the 1ˢᵗ dragoon Regt.

BATAILLONS DE FLOTTILLE ET DE HAUT BORD

1805-1814 Fleet and topside battalions

1805-1814 Nantes guard of honor

Epaulette de chasseur d'infanterie, premier Empire.

Sabretache d'officier du 9ᵉ hussards (1ᵉʳ Empire).

Plaque d'officier de santé Garde Impériale.

1806 Infantry chasseur shoulder, 1805-1814 Officers sabretache of the 9ᵗʰ hussars, 1805-1814 Officer imperial guard badge

1805-1814 Timpanist of the grenadiers cavalry

QUARTIER-MAITRE
DU 10ᵉ RÉGIMENT DE CHASSEURS A CHEVAL.

1806 Bureau officer of 10th Regt. of horse chassseur

Shako du 17ᵉ régiment d'Infanterie de ligne (1807).

Fontes de selle de l'adjoint à l'État-Major général.
(1ᵉʳ Empire.)

1806-1814 Shako of the 17th line infantry, 1806 Saddle cast iron of the deputy general staff

1806-1808 Northern legion

1806-1812 Drummers of the 3rd Swiss Regt.

1806-1812 3rd Swiss Regt.: grandier and chasseaur

1806-1812 Musicians of the 3rd Swiss Regt.

3ᵉ RÉGIMENT SUISSE. — SAPEUR.

1806-1812 Sapper of the 3rd Swiss Regt.

TROMPETTE DU 9e HUSSARDS, COMPAGNIES ORDINAIRES (1806-1812).

1806-1812 Trumpet of the 9th hussars, ordinary companies

1807 Assistants of the vice President Alexandre Berthier, Prince of Neuchatel, Major General

CHASSEUR-VOLTIGEUR DE LA GARDE DE PARIS (1807).

1807 Chasseaur-voltigeur of the 2nd Regt. of the Paris guard

OFFICIERS DE GRENADIERS D'INFANTERIE DE LIGNE (1ᵉʳ EMPIRE)

1807 Line infantry grenadier officers

1807 Officers of voltigeurs and chasseurs of light infantry

1807 Trumpet of the Arenberg light cavalry

1807-1812 Drums of the 15th light infantry Regt.

1807-1812 Light infantry bar holder

1808 A.d.C. of the Marechal, Prince of Ponte-Corvo and Bernadotte's son

1808 Honorary guard of Senat

J. D'ALEMAN, CAPITAINE DE LA GARDE D'HONNEUR DE BAYONNE (1808).

1808 Jean d'Aleman, captain of honor guard on foot in the city of Bayonne

MARÉCHAL DES LOGIS, CHEF DES SAPEURS
DU 30ᵉ RÉGIMENT DE DRAGONS

1808 Sapper-marechal de logis of 30th dragoon Regt.

1808 Sergeant major of fusiliers of the 2nd Regt. of the Paris guard

1808-1814 Vistula legion infantry

1809 Hussar, lancer, dragoon and royal guard chasseaur in undress

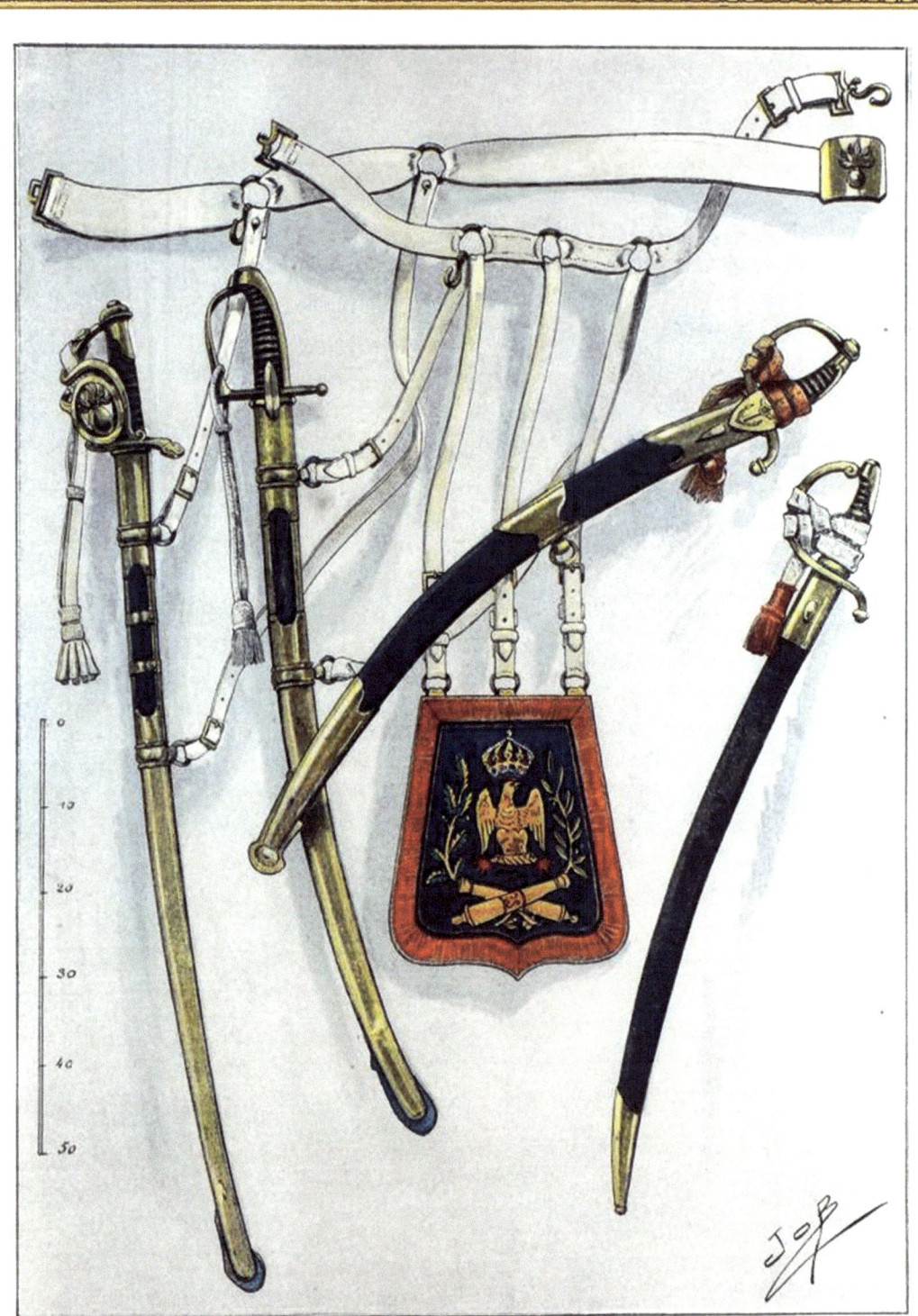

1809 Imperial guard swords

1809 Musicians of the 1st legion of the North national guard

TAMBOUR DU 42ᵉ RÉGIMENT D'INFANTERIE (1809).

1809 Drum of the 42nd infantry Regt.

TROMPETTES DU 2ᵉ RÉGIMENT DE HUSSARDS

(D'après les gouaches de la Bibliothèque du Ministère de la Guerre)

1809 Trumpets of 2nd hussar Regt.

AIDE DE CAMP DE MARÉCHAL DE FRANCE
(Premier Empire)

1810 A.d.C. of a French marshal

ARTILLERIE DU BATAILLON DE NEUCHATEL EN 1810

1810 Artillery of the Neuchatel battalion

GRENADIER DE LA GARDE IMPÉRIALE EN TENUE DE ROUTE

1810 Grenadier of the old imperial guard

GARDES-CÔTES
(1810)

1810 Guard of sea cost

1810 Vétérinaires of artillery and cavalry corps

ARTILLERIE A PIED DE LA GARDE IMPÉRIALE
Tenue d'été, revue du dimanche.

1811 Artillery on foot of the imperial guard

ADJUDANT SOUS-OFFICIER — MARÉCHAL-DES-LOGIS CHEF — ÉLÈVES DE LA 3ᵉ Cⁱᵉ
ÉCOLE DE CAVALERIE DE SAINT-GERMAIN

1811 Cavalry school of Saint-Germain

TAMBOUR-MAJOR ET MUSICIEN D'INFANTERIE DE LIGNE EN TENUE DE CAMPAGNE
(1ᵉʳ EMPIRE, AVANT 1812)

1811 Drum major and line infantry musician in field uniform

TROMPETTE-MAJOR
DE L'ÉCOLE DE CAVALERIE DE SAINT-GERMAIN

1811 Major trumpet of cavalry school of Saint-Germain

1811 Trumpets of the 14th, 23rd and 24th Regt. of horse chasseaur

1812 Artillery on foot

1812 Eagle holder

OFFICIER DES CHASSEURS A CHEVAL DE LA GARDE, 1er EMPIRE
(D'après un portrait du temps. Collection de M. Job.)

1812 Officer of the chasseurs of the imperial guard

1812 Trumpet of carabiniers

1812 Trumpets of light cavalry

**BRIGADIER TROMPETTE DU TRAIN
ET TROMPETTE DU 1ᵉʳ BATAILLON DU TRAIN DES ÉQUIPAGES
(1812)**

1812 Trumpets of equipment train

GARDE D'ARTILLERIE

(1812-1814)

1812-1814 Artillery guard

FOURRIER DU 11ᵉ HUSSARDS EN TENUE DE BAL — HUSSARD DU 9ᵉ RÉGIMENT

1812-1814 Hussar an fourier of 9ᵗʰ and 11ᵗʰ Regt.

FUSILIER DU 4ᵉ RÉGIMENT D'INFANTERIE DE LIGNE

EN TENUE DE ROUTE

1812-1815 Fusilier of 4th line infantry Regt.

1813 General commanding of the guard of honour

OFFICIER D'ORDONNANCE DE L'EMPEREUR (TENUE DE CAMPAGNE).

1813 Emperor's ordinatory officer in field uniform

1815 Napoleon at Waterloo

SOLDIERS, WEAPONS & UNIFORMS ALREADY PUBLISHED
(SOME TITLES)

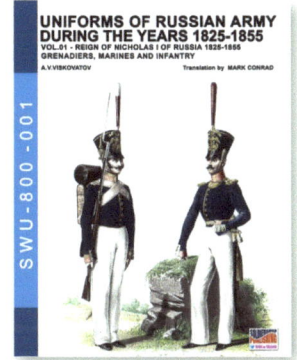
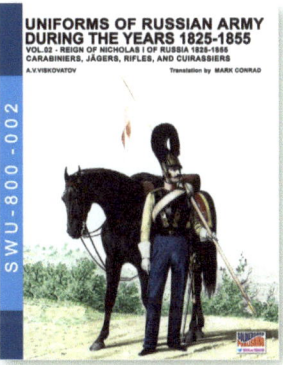
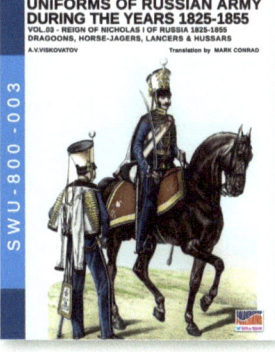
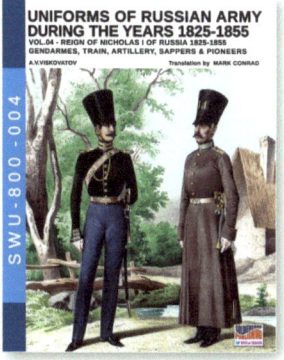
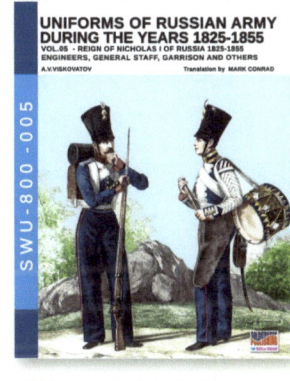
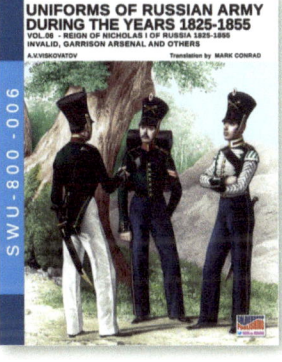
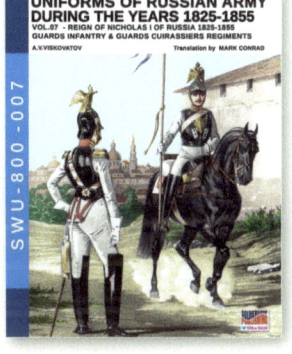
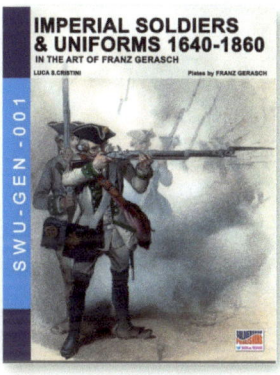
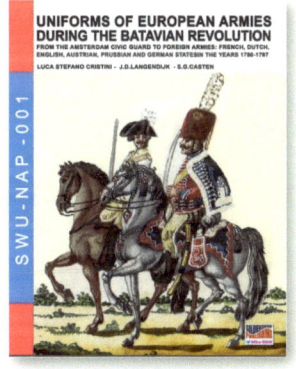

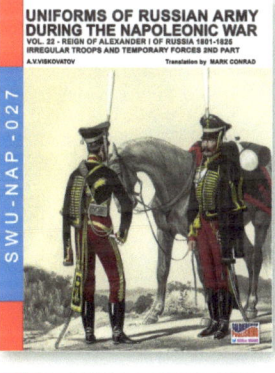
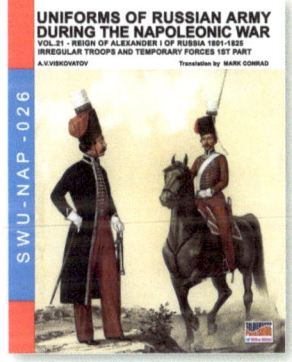

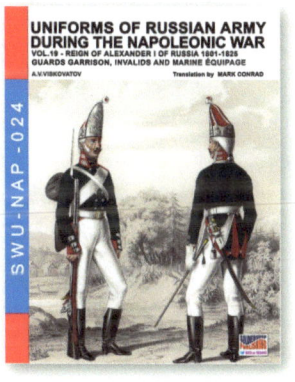
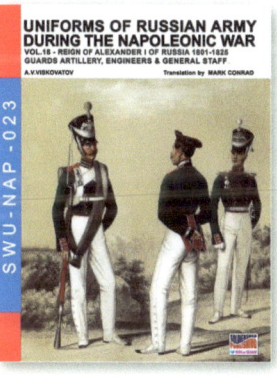

www.ingramcontent.com/pod-product-compliance
Lightning Source LLC
Chambersburg PA
CBHW041524220426
43669CB00003B/39